THE
POWER
OF
FAITH

Living by Faith

EMMERENTIA NUPA ASAFOR

Copyright

The Power of Faith

© Emmerentia Nupa Asafor 2018

All rights reserved.

No part of this book may be reproduced, stored in a retrieval system, or transmitted in any form or by any means - electronic, mechanical, recording, or otherwise- without the prior written permission of the author.

Emmerentia Nupa Asafor

DEDICATION

To all my loved ones who have departed from this world

We will Meet again

In Heaven

INTRODUCTION

For my many years, as a Christian and believer, I have come to realize that one of the greatest challenges we believers face is the lack of trust in God in the face of adversity. Our faith is shaken and soon gives way to fear. We worship God and sing praise songs when He blesses us, but have difficulties standing and singing the same songs when life gets tough and things don't go the way we expect. What we forget is that He is the same God in times of joy as well as times of sorrow. So why don't we learn to praise God even when the ground under our feet is giving way, and we are in tears, or when all hope is gone? It is not easy but by faith we can grow to know that praising God is not determined by our circumstances. We ought to praise and worship Him for who He is not for what He does for us.

It is a normal human reaction to tremble, to complain, and question God in the face of challenges. We often say: "Why me? Why now? Where is God? Can He hear me? For how long do I have to wait? Does He really love me? How long does He want me to feel this pain? But He said He will never leave me nor forsake me!"

Sometimes we will reach out to others to pray for us

which is good if we trust the person's spiritual standing since the Bible states that when two decree a thing on earth God will agree with them in Heaven. But remember you know your problem best;- you have a personal relationship with God, and you can argue your case with God better than anyone else. It's sad and unfortunate to note that some Christians go as far as consulting other gods out of fear and lack of trust in God Almighty. When they do this, they become vulnerable and can easily fall into the trap of the demonic kingdom. God is greatly displeased by this behavior because He is a jealous God and will never share His glory with anyone.

Frankly speaking, most of us have been through pain, hardship, humiliation, failure, rejection, and persecution: bitter experiences which not only weaken our faith but give the enemy the opportunity to come in and torment us knowing we live in fear and doubt. On the other hand, God is not happy when we let fear replace our faith. We just have to believe that nothing is too hard for Him and keep trusting Him.

What inspired me to write this book was the fact that I often found myself asking these same questions that I hear other brothers and sisters asking. I came to realize that I could dive deep into the Word of God to look at the lives of other men and women of faith and see how God helped them through their wilderness experiences. The Bible tells us in the book of Daniel chapter 7 and verse 9 that God is the Ancient of days, so what He was able to do for Abraham in his old age, for Daniel, Shadrach, Meshach, and Abednego or for the woman with the issue of blood, He can do it for you and me today. The common denominator in these examples is that they had faith and believed that God had the power to safe and heal. For 12 years the woman with the issue of blood never gave up. She kept looking for an opportunity to meet Jesus. She finally got her miracle. What about you? How long have you been waiting for your miracle? I come today to encourage you to keep trusting, praising, worshipping, and believing, for we serve a big God.

Today, I can attest to the fact that since I started spending more time meditating the Word of God during hard times, I have gone closer to God and I have grown to love and trust Him more. He has never failed me. I look for scriptures in the bible that align with the problem I am facing, meditate on these passages, with praise and worship and then I wait attentively upon the Lord to give me direction on how to solve the problem. I believe in miracles, but I also know that God uses the people around us to do most of the miracles in our lives. Having faith in God is a process, and like every process, you know exactly what the outcome will be. **God is faithful!**

It is this personal experience with God that I would like to share with many Christians that I believe are going through or have been through the same struggles like me in their Christian life. This is for those children of God who have acknowledged His love for them, and therefore, hunger and thirst for a very intimate relationship with Him.

This is not just another book you are about to read. This is God reaching out to you through this book. I trust that by the time you get to the last page you will experience a fresh touch of God. As you read on, I pray for you: that the Spirit of God through these pages will not only increase your faith but will take you to higher heights in every area of your life so that He can use you to bring the light of God to those who are still living in darkness. PEACE!

CHAPTER ONE

What is Faith?

The Merriam Webster's Student dictionary provides the following definitions of Faith:

*Devotion to duty or a person **or** loyalty; the quality of keeping one's promises; belief and trust in and loyalty to God; belief in the doctrines of a religion; firm belief even in the absence of proof; complete confidence; something that is firmly believed, especially a system of religious beliefs.*

What is Faith for you and me, as followers of Christ?

Faith is both a spiritual substance and force that connects us to God and permits us to communicate with God on the basis of trust. It is our faith that moves us to pray every day; to get up on Sundays and go to church knowing our leader is a priest or pastor in human form like us. So what does faith mean for us?

The book of Hebrews chapter 11:1(KJV) states:

"Now faith is the substance of things hoped for, the evidence of things not seen."

The Power of Faith

In real life we want to see before we believe, Scientists want to prove every law before they approve it for application. Here we know we are dealing with God Almighty, the one who made Heaven and Earth; the one we cannot see. It will only take faith to enter into a relationship with God and to remain faithful to Him in everything we do.

Faith means that we are fully convinced of the truthfulness and reliability of that in which we believe. This means that our walk as Christians cannot take us far if we don't have faith.

When we set out on a journey, our desire is to go from point A, where the journey starts, to point B, where it ends. Our destination as Christians is Heaven where we will meet Christ and rejoice with Him forever. No journey can be accomplished if the car we are driving stays on the same spot, or the plane we board refuses to take off. Similarly, every day of our Christian lives is a land mark on the faith journey, and the things we say or do, the way we react to the obstacles we meet on the way can accelerate the journey, slow it down, or bring it to a complete halt.

We are blessed because we have a book of reference. The Bible is the platform from which we communicate with God through faith. There is nothing you and I are going through today that cannot be referenced in the Bible. The same way God brought each one of the believers in the Bible out of their predicament or the difficult situations they found themselves in, is the same way He will do it for you and me today. The Bible tells us believers, followers of Christ in Hebrews 13:8: (KJV)

"Jesus Christ the same yesterday, and today, and forever."

Our Lord and Master has not changed, and He is willing to do anything for you and me, especially when we call upon Him in Faith. He is a loving and faithful God; no one has ever called upon Him according to His word and has been ignored or put to shame. He is not happy when we call upon Him with doubt because that can mean that we undermine His omnipotence. The Bible emphasizes this in Hebrews 11:6(KJV)

"But without faith it is impossible to please him: for he that cometh to God must believe that he is, and that he is a rewarder of them that diligently seek him."

There is a constant battle between reason and faith in the minds of most Christians, but faith always wins because God will make sure He defends those who call upon His name. Therefore, we should learn to stand firm in the midst of all the storms of life. When we seek God Almighty, we should refrain from seeking other gods or putting other people in His place.

When God moves, He moves alone, He does not need help from man to do whatever He wants to do. He spoke the world into existence. He did not need man to help Him arrange the seas, the oceans, the mountains, the planets, the valleys, the sun, the moon, and the stars. It is true that He can use people to bless us or get us out of certain intricate situations but if you have a discerning spirit you will see God's hand at work every step of the way. He will send people in our lives to find solutions to our problems but we should always be careful enough to give the glory back to Him and learn to see His handwork in each individual that shows up in such times of need in order to make true the word in Jeremiah 29:11 (KJV):

"For I know the thoughts that I think toward you, saith the Lord, thoughts of peace, and not of evil, to give you an expected end."

Sometimes, God seems to place us, His children, in a place of extreme difficulty. Such situations and circumstances should not make us question God's love for us or even His very existence. On the contrary, it is at this time that we need to stretch our faith and pray without ceasing. If we have the ability to solve every single problem we encounter, then God will cease to be God. When we have our backs on the wall, when we have exhausted our human strength, intelligence, and ruse, then God shows up in grand style. He comes in as the owner of the universe, the creator, the one in charge, to portray His supernatural power and pour out abundant grace to make us smile again. In the Christian life, faith and works go together like inhaling and exhaling. Billy Graham stated it in these terms: *Faith is taking the Gospel in; works is taking the Gospel out.*

Standing in the Storms.

We refer to Abraham as the father of our faith because by faith Abraham, when he was called to go to a place he didn't know, he obeyed and went out, not knowing exactly where he was going. Hebrews 11:8 (KJV) He trusted God even to the point of giving up an only son:

"And it came to pass after these things, which God did tempt Abraham, and said unto him, Abraham: and he said, Behold, here I am

2 And he said, Take now thy son, thine only son Isaac, whom thou lovest, and get thee into the land of Moriah; and offer him there for a burnt offering upon one of the mountains which I will tell thee of.3 And Abraham rose up early in the morning, and saddled his ass, and took two of his young men with him, and Isaac his son, and clave the wood for the burnt offering, and rose up, and went unto the place of which God had told him". Gen 22:1-3(KJV)

The fact that he had total confidence in God made him accept offering up Isaac, his only begotten son, a son he waited so long to receive from God.Genesis22:2(KJV). God not only provided a lamb to Abraham for the sacrifice after testing him but blessed him mightily through his son Isaac. God looks at our hearts, and when He sees that our hearts have been completely yielded to Him, like was the case with Abraham, then He is able and willing to sign us an open check. Many of us have children so we can relate to Abraham as a parent.

He had only one child that he loved, Isaac, the promised child. We also know that Ishmael was not the promised child, and that he and his mother had to go away from Abraham's house. It was a very tough decision for Abraham to accept to do God's will by sacrificing his only son. It was because of his love for God and the faith he had. He was ready to lose his son because he was convinced that it was better to obey God and lose a son than to disobey God. None of us today would be willing to take the risk Abraham took, even if it meant sacrificing only one of our numerous children. However, when we get to that place of faith where we trust God foolishly, then such faith will be the reason for God to move in a very spectacular and miraculous manner in our lives.

The Bible says that obedience is better than sacrifice. God looks at our hearts, and because he saw in Abraham's heart that he was ready to sacrifice Isaac, He provided a lamb for the sacrifice. God keeps a record of everything we do for Him. He alone is able to reward us for our obedience and sacrifices.

"Again by faith, God made the Israelites pass through the Red Sea as by dry land: but when the Egyptians tried to cross they drowned. By faith the walls of Jericho fell down, after they were compassed about seven days." Hebrews 11:29-31(KJV)

The above examples emphasize the role that faith plays in our Christian journey. Are you facing a Red Sea situation in your life? Is there a huge wall separating you from your place of victory?

What are you doing to make God speak to you the way He did to Abraham and to the Israelites? Have you truly accepted Him as your Lord and Savior? Are you living a life that glorifies Him? Can you stand in any crowd and declare without restraint that Christ is all you live for? Have you turned away from sinful habits just because you don't want to break your relationship with God? This is the time for us to answer these questions honestly and seek to strengthen the bond between us and God through prayer. By so doing, we will make room for Christ to dwell in us and shatter every plan of the enemy in our lives.

God existed before the universe, and the fact is that God does not change, has never changed, and will never change. He is the unchangeable changer. He provided wine at the marriage feast in Cana, bread and fish to the multitudes in the desert, a lamb to Abraham on mount Mariah, so He will provide for you in every situation: be it your health, your finances, your shattered family situation, your marriage, your immigration situation, your job, your promotion, and every desire of your heart. Our God is more than able. The Bible says this in Ephesians 3:20 (KJV)

"Now to Him who is able to do exceedingly abundantly above all that we ask or think, according to the power that works in us."

The power that works in us here refers to our faith, which releases the blessings of God. So let us ask God for the grace to increase our faith, which will in turn, release the power of God in our lives.

Chapter Two

Jesus, the Author and Finisher of My Faith

"For God so loved the world, that he gave his only begotten Son, that whosoever believeth in him should not perish, but have everlasting life." John 3:16 (KJV)

"23 For all have sinned, and come short of the glory of God;" Romans 3:23(KJV)

"23 For the wages of sin is death; but the gift of God is eternal life through Jesus Christ our Lord." Romans 6:23 (KJV)

"8 But God commendeth his love toward us, in that, while we were yet sinners, Christ died for us." Romans 5:8 (KJV)

We were supposed to perish or suffer death because we sinned against God, but God sent His only son to die in order to reconcile us to Him. Jesus Christ could have refused to die this shameful and humiliating death ,but He accepted to be nailed to the cross for the love of you and me. In order for us to enjoy the benefits of the coming of the Son of God, we must believe. If we live a life of unbelief, fear, and doubt, the sacrifice Jesus made on Calvary will not yield any fruit in our lives. This belief then turns into faith which is a whole process.

"⁸For by grace are ye saved through faith; and that not of yourselves: it is the gift of God:

⁹Not of works, lest any man should boast" Ephesians 2:8-9 (KJV)

Every day comes with new challenges and by constantly reminding ourselves of the promises in the word of God, and daily reviving our faith, we are able to stay strong. God gave us the gift of faith. It is by activating it, and making it grow ,that we can overcome the trials, temptations, and tribulations that confront us.

Christ's death was an act of obedience, love, humility, sacrifice, and courage. It was at this point that our faith journey began. Jesus invited us to believe in order to live the abundant life that He purchased for us through his belittling death and glorious resurrection. The devil comes to kill to steal, and to destroy, but Jesus came to destroy his works and give us the more abundant life that He promised us in John 10:10.How many times in our daily Christian lives do we remember to carry out acts of obedience, love, humility, sacrifice, and courage to emulate Him as the author and finisher of our faith? How often do we show appreciation to our savior for what He did for us? We tend to say that He was able to do all what He did because He was both God and man. This is true, but it is also stated:

"And Jesus said unto them, Because of your unbelief: for verily I say unto you, If ye have faith as a grain of mustard seed, ye shall say unto this mountain, Remove hence to yonder place; and it shall remove; and nothing shall be impossible unto you." Mathew 17:20 (KJV)

Faith is the vehicle that will take us through our journey with God. The Word of God is the fuel this vehicle will need to accomplish this journey. Without faith we are not likely to get to our destination. If we stay plugged into the Word of God, if we have a strong determination, we will not only persist in the race but we will finish the race. The word of God will help us overcome every obstacle along the way and lead us to our final destination. The hurdles may be uncountable, but the grace of God through faith is more than sufficient to carry us through.

What are the things Jesus did in His Ministry to demonstrate and strengthen His faith? Although He was both God and man, He taught His disciples how to carry on with the Ministry after He would have gone back to His Father. First, Jesus called His disciples, and then He said He would make them fishers of men. As Christians, our faith should be grounded on the great commission to preach the gospel to the whole world.

"Go ye therefore, and teach all nations, baptizing them in the name of the Father, and of the Son, and of the Holy Ghost:

Teaching them to observe all things whatsoever I have commanded you: and, lo, I am with you always, even unto the end of the world. Amen." Matthew 28:19-20 (KJV)

Everyone that comes in contact with us should experience Jesus in the way we talk to them, minister to their needs, and show compassion to the suffering. Jesus taught His disciples how to pray. Our faith is the bridge that links us to our Heavenly Father, and prayer is the vehicle that takes us back and forth on this bridge to communicate with our Father. It is this frequent communication that inspires, strengthens, empowers, and increases us.

In Jesus' Ministry, we have numerous accounts of how He healed the sick, fed the hungry, comforted the afflicted, gave drink to the thirsty, and set the captives free. What are we doing to help the sick not only in our families but also in our church communities, at work, and in our neighborhoods? What words do we speak to a hurting person? Are they comforting words? Are they the same words Christ would speak if He met that person? Have we extended a helping hand to an elderly person in the store, on the bus, on the train or everywhere else? Have we deprived ourselves of one meal or drink because someone near us needed it more? How often do we give sacrificially? Some people give to boost their ego and feel important. God will not reward you for such selfish giving. The Bible says when we give we should not allow our left hand see what is in our right hand. We should give like Jesus gave each time He ministered to a sick person: out of compassion and love.

There are many hurting people out on the streets and

in the hospitals, but a lot of times our ministry starts inside the church and ends inside the church. This can be very misleading as those who need more help are yet to find their way to church. These are the people we Christians should go after. Let's identify these people and begin to help transform their lives one after the other. God will grant us the grace and the means to carry out this divine assignment.

Chapter Three

Faith Kept Me When They Turned Their Backs on Me.

There is hardly any one among us who has not been through betrayal in their lives. Sometimes things get so bad that you ask yourself if life is worth living. The same people you gave up time, material, and energy to minister to their needs turn around and say very evil things about you and paint false pictures of you to everyone around them.

Are you the wife whose husband has turned his back on you or vise-versa? Marriage was ordained in heaven. It is important that Jesus Christ be brought into every marriage. He will sustain your marriage if you consecrate it to Him and constantly pray to Him as a family. Make Him the custodian of your marriage, and He will chase every intruder away and renew your love for each other as you enthrone Him as Lord in your home. The presence of God is what transforms a house into a home.

Are you the mother whose children have refused to listen to you or appreciate the sacrifices you made to get them to where they are in life? Do these children treat you like trash? Have you spent sleepless nights crying because the very children you carried in your womb, showered them with love, and provided for them, scandalized you and called you horrible names? You are not alone. Refer them to the word of God:

[1]"Children, obey your parents in the Lord: for this is right.

[2]Honour thy father and mother; which is the first commandment with promise;

[3]That it may be well with thee, and thou mayest live long on the earth." Ephesians 6:1-3 (KJV)

You may also be like Joseph whose siblings, out of jealousy, hated him, plotted against him, sold him as a slave, and even proclaimed his death to his father. Or yet still, you may be that hard worker who is never appreciated by your supervisor, whose promotion has been held down for years upon years. Are you the student whose teacher is giving you bad grades because of some selfish and hidden motive?

Take your complaints to God who is the author and finisher of your faith. He has the solution to every problem.

Are you sick in your body and feel discouraged because you think there is no hope for you? Hear the word of God:

"And ye shall serve the LORD your God, and he shall bless thy bread, and thy water; and I will take sickness away from the midst of thee." Exodus 23:25 (KJV)

As Christians we all go through many challenges in our lives. The unbelievers and atheists are equally confronted with such difficulties but the advantage we have as Christians is that we have the word of God to stand upon. We also know by faith that Christ obtained victory for us over two thousand years ago on the cross of Calvary. It is by faith that we can begin to declare the Word of God over every situation in order to appropriate the already acquired victory. Fear will not do it for us, grumbling will not do it for us, and talking about it without inviting God into the situation will only make things worse.

"Many *are* the afflictions of the righteous: but the LORD delivereth him out of them all." Psalm 34:19(KJV)

Our daily lives are certainly plagued by horrendous experiences that sometimes take us to rock bottom. One thing is guaranteed; our victory is having faith in the finished work of the cross. God assures us that He will deliver us from all our afflictions, and I know all means without any exception. This is the reason why I love and trust God beyond measure. My faith in Him is bigger than my mind can fathom. This reassurance keeps me going, refuels my spiritual engine to continue the journey to heaven which is my ultimate destination. I trust and pray the same for you as you read through these pages.

When we raise a petition to God, we should rest assured that He is a prayer answering God and begin to thank Him before the answer ever gets to us. By adopting this attitude, we are preventing the enemy from establishing strongholds in our minds when we worry and fear about the future.

The Power of Faith

"Be careful for nothing; but in everything by prayer and supplication with thanksgiving let your requests be made known unto God.

[7] And the peace of God, which passeth all understanding, shall keep your hearts and minds through Christ Jesus." Philippians 4:6-7(KJV)

Chapter Four

How Do We Exercise Our Faith in Our Daily Lives?

God is interested in Families and the proof is that He put Adam and Eve in the Garden of Eden as the first family. The Bible says in 1 Peter 5:8 (KJV):

"Be sober, be vigilant; because your adversary the devil, as a roaring lion, walketh about, seeking whom he may devour:"

The devil is always attacking families because his plan is to destroy every good thing that God put in place.

"The thief cometh not, but for to steal, and to kill, and to destroy: I am come that they might have life, and that they might have it more abundantly." John 10:10 (KJV)

Jesus is the Good Shepherd that laid His life on the cross for us, His sheep. Therefore, we should dedicate our families to Jesus because at the mention of the name of Jesus, Satan and his agents will flee from our families. As Christians, we should not put our faith in man to solve problems in our families. No man can do what God can do. If we are going through trouble in our families with our parents, our children, our spouses, or our siblings, there is only one person that can identify and solve every kind of problem. You must take it to Him believing that He is omnipresent, omniscient, and omnipotent. Very often, humans intervene to solve problems for us: let's learn to ask God through the Holy Spirit to speak through these persons. This is how we live our faith. God will use people to help us, but we must submit the problem to Him and ask Him to send us helpers. He knows and can choose the best people to help us out of each complicated situation.

When your car breaks down, you take it to the shop that is specialized in that make of car because they conceived that car and are therefore in a better position to diagnose and solve the problem .The same is true with God. He made us and it was His plan for us to enjoy good health, peace, and love in our families. He created us, so He can recreate our body parts or transform the sick or damaged parts. He has the power and the authority to kick the devil out, set us free, and restore a peace that surpasses all understanding.

Today, we live in a stress plagued society. We worry about our bills, our health, our careers, and our families. We work very hard to earn a living and to keep our jobs. However, God alone has the ability to sustain our jobs and this is why we should work to please God not man. God is proud of us when we do the right thing and portray a good reputation as His children. Whatever we do, we should be aware that God is watching us. Remember that God does not only look at our hearts, but He knows our motives. Do your job to please God, and He will be there to fight for you when that unfair supervisor gives you a bad evaluation. He will be there to answer the query you got simply because you did not satisfy your supervisor's desires outside of your work schedule. The Bible says that the arm of flesh will fail you, so you ought to respect your supervisors at your job, but do not see them like small gods, and do not believe that your elevation will come from them. The Bible tells us that promotion comes from God, and when you do your work such that it is pleasing to God, He will put your name on your supervisor's table in due time.

In our health, God is the greatest healer. Doctors cure, but God heals. It has never been His wish for any of us to suffer pain.

"But he was wounded for our transgressions; he was bruised for our iniquities: the chastisement of our peace was upon him; and with his stripes we are healed."

Isaiah 53:5(KJV)

There are so many instances in the Bible when Jesus came across the sick and was moved with so much compassion that He could not let them go with their afflictions. Let's examine the following examples:

"And, behold, they brought to him a man sick of the palsy, lying on a bed: and Jesus seeing their faith said unto the sick of the palsy; Son, be of good cheer; thy sins be forgiven thee." Matthew 9:2(KJV)

What catches my attention here are the words "Jesus seeing their faith" and; "thy sins be forgiven thee". Faith is highlighted here as a prerequisite for the man's healing. Also, by telling the man that his sins are forgiven and expecting him to be healed implies that some illnesses can afflict us as a result of our sinful lifestyle. Therefore, we should always ask God for the grace to hate sin and love God, and love our neighbors, too, by doing good to them as commanded by God.

When we feed the hungry, we are making God happy. Sometimes, a simple drink to the thirsty can open great doors for us. So when we open our doors to strangers, we are serving God. When we refuse to visit the sick in hospitals or those locked up in the prisons, we are telling God that the blood He shed on Calvary was not for them. His heart is after the hurting. He handed over the responsibility and the power to us before going up to heaven.

"For I was an hungred, and ye gave me meat: I was thirsty, and ye gave me drink: I was a stranger, and ye took me in: Naked, and ye clothed me: I was sick, and ye visited me: I was in prison, and ye came unto me." Matthew25:35-36(KJV)

"And Jesus went about all Galilee, teaching in their synagogues, and preaching the gospel of the kingdom, and healing all manner of sickness and all manner of disease among the people." Matthew 4:23 (KJV)

In the above passage, the Bible tells us that Jesus went about healing all manner of sickness and all manner of disease among people. Good health is one of the biggest blessings we can pray for. Our blessings are not only financial. We cannot function normally in poor health. You often hear people talking about the wealthiest people but very rarely do people talk about the healthiest people or the most god fearing people. Yet, these are the people that are most likely to spend eternity with God. Our life does not end here and the proof is that death has no fear for riches or power. The rich and the poor end up the same way, and this is why it is important to reflect on the life we want to live after death because no human being has succeeded in solving the mystery of death. This notwithstanding, death does not always result from sickness. Sometimes our initial reaction when we hear someone has cancer or any other disease that western medicine labels as terminal is to conclude that the person is about to die. As Christians, we should step in, activate our faith, and join it to that of the sick person and pray for God to intervene even while we are following up with medical treatment. God's power is beyond our imagination and unless we begin to call upon Him with that trust that He can do more than our minds can contain, we are not preparing the ground for spectacular miracles. When we go to God, we must eliminate every element of doubt.

Our heavenly Father is interested in our total well-being, which includes our finances. He wants us to be self-sufficient. He has given us the power to create wealth, so if we work hard and live according to His statutes, we should reap the fruits of our labor. Always remember that nothing we have comes from us; all what we have belongs to God, so when we are blessed, it is to be a blessing to others. God likes us to share what we have with the suffering and the needy. If we don't have materials to share, we can share our time with the sick, praying for them and helping them experience the love of God through our visits and prayers.

Christians believe in life after death. This is a good thing about our faith because no matter the trials, tribulations, and temptations we face in this life, there is hope for a better life and a reason for us to keep living a righteous life here on Earth.

God has commanded us to take this message of hope to every living soul so that they should not perish. No father wants any of his children to perish. The same goes for our Heavenly Father.

"And Jesus came and spake unto them, saying, All power is given unto me in heaven and in earth.

Go ye therefore, and teach all nations, baptizing them in the name of the Father, and of the Son, and of the Holy Ghost:" (Matthew 28:18-19 KJV).

Many people are still living in ignorance, so those of us that God has called as laborers should bring the light of Christ to all the areas where darkness still prevails. Our influence should reach where people still believe in all kinds of evil powers rather than in the supreme and supernatural power of God. We are mandated to carry out the great commission starting with our families, to our communities, our countries, and the world at large, as we await the coming of our Lord and Savior.

Chapter Five

My Family, My Pillar of Faith.

I was actually born into a catholic family. My late father, Papa Joseph Asafor, alias Pa Teacher, was a catholic teacher all his life. My parents were very devoted catholics and my siblings and I grew up doing everything that catholics do. We all learned to pray and loved to pray. I got baptized as a baby at the age of two weeks. I received First Holy Communion and Confirmation before going to secondary school. On Sunday mornings, my father would make sure we all left the house at the same time to walk four miles to the Catholic Church in Akum.

I come from a family of eight. There are two males :Cornelius and Emmanuel ,and six females: Isabella ,Immaculate, Florence, Joan ,Evangeline, and my humble self Emmerentia, who by chance was born first. I am thankful to God because the Christian education we got from our parents has yielded fruit. We are all Christians and believers today and try to practice our faith and live godly lives. We are far from perfect, but we pray every day for God's grace. We teach our children the value of believing in God and according Him the place He deserves in our lives in the way we interact with others. This way, we encourage them to spread the light of God into the lives of those they meet and help carry out the great assignment of leading everyone to Christ. Each time we get together as a family for any occasion, we are careful to give God chairmanship of our reunion. We have been through a lot of difficulties and trials as a family; we have never stopped trusting God, and when we look back today, we can only say "Thank you, Lord for always being there for us."

Once again, I remain forever grateful for the seed of faith my parents sowed into my life, and this explains why growing up as a young girl I had so much love for God and enjoyed serving in church. While a student in **Our Lady of Lourdes Secondary School** in Bamenda, Cameroon, I was taught to pray more intensive catholic prayers by the reverend sisters who ran the school. I woke up every morning at 5 a.m. to get ready for mass, and I never looked for excuses to stay away from morning mass even when it was very cold. I can trace my love for God back to that early age, or to better put it, God's love for me. I made a place for Him in my heart. As a young girl I was part of the Focolare Movement founded by Chiara Lubich in Italy. This is an international organization that promotes the ideals of unity and universal brotherhood. Their base in Cameroon is in Fontem in the Lebialem County of Southern Cameroons. I remember spending a couple of summer holidays with this community doing some volunteer work and praying most of the time for peace and unity in the world. It was a life changing experience for me and took my love for God and humanity one step higher.

I continued in the Catholic Church until about 15 years

ago when I completely embraced the pentecostal movement. During these my years in the catholic church, I was a member of the CWA (Catholic Women's Association). My love for God was still visible in my dedication and participation in the activities of this association. In the Saint Anthony's Catholic Church in Kumba, I would lead the "Stations of the Cross" during lent.

My late husband Mr. Nupa John Simplice, was the music leader in St. Anthony's catholic church Buea Road, Kumba. His musical talent was very unique and his death on September 15th 2008 shocked not only me, my children and the family but the church community as well. The vacuum he left is still to be filled. But God has held my hand with my children and directed us every single step of the way. Today, I speak of the Almighty God, the one who made Heaven and Earth, the one who holds the whole world in His hands. I have known Him since I was born, and I can unequivocally state that **God is faithful**. In my family, in the life of my children, in my life, He has been God in the good times and still God in the bad times. I give Him all the glory.

My mother was a strong believer, and we always went to church as a family. After my father died, I discovered that my mother became a more prayerful person. Her faith rose to a higher level as she was then aware of the fact that she was left alone to take care of both our material and spiritual needs. She was fundamentally a catholic and could be seen all the time with her rosary in her hand, especially when she went to bed and at 5a.m. My mother's prayers helped us children rise to great heights. Not only did she say her rosary several times a day but she made very positive confessions about the power of God, the faithfulness of God, and the fact that God was a prayer answering God. She would always tell me that God hears her when she speaks to Him. She decreed the protection of God upon us and spoke very confidently of the fact that no witch or wizard could mess with any of her children because God almighty was watching over them. Although my mother buried my beloved sister Immaculate, we all went through the pain believing that it was God's plan for my sister's life. My sister's death did not weaken my mother's faith. She lived with that pain but never allowed it to separate her from the love of her God. She, instead, prayed harder for God to preserve the remaining seven children, and her wish was granted until she went to be with the Lord.

If I have great faith in God today, it is thanks to my mother. Her unwavering faith helped to grow mine, and today, I understand the importance of praying for my children and decreeing positive blessings into their lives, thanks to my mother's example. She taught me that you do not have to bless your children only when they were doing the right thing or being nice to you. She taught me that you don't only have to expect gifts from your grown children as is the case with most parents in our culture. My mother gave us gifts especially of money all the time. She always gave me money to take to all my children, her grandchildren.

We went through a lot of hardship, pain, criticism, betrayal, tribulations, and persecutions in our early life with our parents' struggles but I remember that the only place they took us to was to church. I thank God because I have grown up to believe that the only place where problems of every nature and gravity can be solved is the presence of God. The way my mother departed from this world has remained one of the greatest testimonies of my Christian life and greatly boosted my faith.

In November of 2014, I called to chat with my mother from the US, and during our conversation, she asked me if I was planning to travel to Cameroon for Christmas. My response was no because I had no plans to travel. Then she reminded me that she needed me to get her a perfume that I usually got for her. She went further to say that she also wanted a certain cleansing tea. At the end of the conversation, I started thinking of what to do. My initial thought was to send the parcel through any family member that was travelling to Cameroon but by the inspiration of God and my mother's faith, I travelled to Cameroon in December of 2014. I spent time with my mother, sleeping on the same bed, chatting with her, and listening to her humorous stories. She was happy to get the things she had requested from me and I was more than happy to be with her. To me, she was still the strong, energetic, and sweet mother I had always known. My love for her and my refusal to let her go, blinded me to all the visible signs of her departure from this world. Although she looked a little tired, in her usual way she would not let me worry or talk about her situation. She insisted that we pray every night before going to bed. She inquired about all my children, prayed continuously, and released all kinds of blessings upon them but never at any point gave me a clue that she was on her homeward journey.

My return flight to the US was for January 2nd, 2015. She knew I was to go back to the US that day, but I truly believe that the only reason she had wanted me to visit Cameroon was for her to see me and spend some good times with me before her heavenly journey. As she would put it, she always had conversation with God, and I have come to understand that this is the true meaning of prayer. In her conversation with God, she asked that I should not go back to the US without bidding her farewell, so she quietly departed this world on January 1st 2015 on the eve of my scheduled return to the US. One of her best wishes was to depart from this world in the presence of all her children, especially me, the first child of the family, and through her faith God honored her with my presence.

Since her death, I have grown to love and trust God more; I have remained thankful to God for His faithfulness, and pray for a double portion of my mother's faith every day. I made a promise to myself: to hand to my children the same legacy my father and mother handed to us. They were very loving, caring, and giving parents, and the most precious gift they gave us was Jesus Christ.

God blessed my husband and I with six children: Gerald, Ian-Love, Minette, Sidonie, Edward, and Manuela. They were all baptized in the Catholic Church as kids. Today, they all know the degree of my attachment to God, and although they respect my commitment to my faith, they sometimes think I am a fanatic. When they go through challenges , they ask me to pray for them ,and the good thing is that they can attest to the fact that whenever I pray, God answers my prayers. I pray for God to increase their faith and help them develop a close relationship with Him. Each time I go on my knees I pray like Joshua:

"15 And if it seem evil unto you to serve the Lord, choose you this day whom ye will serve; whether the gods which your fathers served that were on the other side of the flood, or the gods of the Amorites, in whose land ye dwell: but as for me and my house, we will serve the Lord." Joshua 24:15 (KJV)

When I was first exposed to the Pentecostal way of worship some 18 years ago, it took me a very long time to stop attending mass in the Catholic Church. Even as a catholic I was not a mere church goer. I reserved a special place for God in my heart. I loved God at a young age even though I was not in a position to explain why. I now understand that it was because He loved me and did not want me to perish, so He embraced me and never let me go. When I look at my spiritual life today, I always thank God that I got born again. I do not have anything against any other denomination because I believe God alone knows who of us is doing what is right in His sight. However, the one thing the Pentecostal Church has done in my life has been to bring me closer to God through intimacy with God's word. It has built my confidence in God.

Growing up, I was never made to know that the Bible was at everyone's disposal and that we could use the Word of God to speak into our daily circumstances. It could have been that in my society at the time there was no means to make the Bible available to everyone as a means to propagate the gospel.

That notwithstanding, my faith in God has grown to the level where I truly believe that as long as I walk according to the will of God, as long as I stand upon His word and seek His face on a daily basis, I carry Him with me in every situation. I know He resists the proud, so I always pray for the grace to continuously humble myself and submit to the will of God. I also trust that I can speak anything according to the Word of God and it shall come to pass because Christ speaks through me. It is my goal to preserve myself as a vessel of honor in order to sustain and enjoy the presence of God. When the spirit of God departs from us, we are empty and helpless. I pray for the grace never to grieve the Holy Spirit, and I pray a prayer of repentance every day to make sure I am in right standing with my Lord and maker. I am also aware of the fact that He will come like a thief, unannounced, so I pray every day to be ready when He comes so that I should not miss my goal, which is heaven.

"For what shall it profit a man, if he shall gain the whole world, and lose his own soul?" Mark 8:36 (KJV)|

"Ye adulterers and adulteresses, know ye not that the friendship of the world is enmity with God? Whosoever therefore will be a friend of the world is the enemy of God." James 4: 4(KJV)

If we want to conform to the way of the world, to do the things that are displeasing to God but are pleasing to man, we are simply preparing a place for ourselves in the pit of hell. We are in the world, but we should not be of the world. We pray for grace and mercy to abide in the Lord.

CHAPTER SIX

Make Your Faith Work for You.

What are our objectives as Christians? For example, a school teacher will state the lesson objectives and read them out loud with the students before they begin the lesson. They state exactly what it is they will accomplish by the end of the lesson. In the course of the lesson the teacher keeps adjusting instruction depending on the response of the students. If they are not responding to questions the way the teacher expects, he/she reformulates them and makes them easier and more comprehensible for the students.

It is the same way our Christian faith should function. We should set spiritual goals for ourselves every day. If we pray for something and don't receive it, we should do self-examination by asking ourselves questions. Are we praying enough? Are we praying the right prayer based on God's word? Is anything blocking our prayers from reaching God? Is there any prince of Persia holding our blessings or answers that have already been released? Do we go to God only to place demands upon Him rather than to fellowship with Him as our Creator and Father?

Can we identify with the one leper that went back to thank Jesus after his healing, or with the nine that went their way and never came back to say thank you? Remember that the one leper who went back to thank Jesus was made whole while the other nine were only healed of leprosy. The same is true today, when we cultivate the habit of thanking God every time , including when things are going wrong, we are telling God that He is in charge of every circumstance in our lives.

This will lure Him to intervene and begin to put things in the right perspective. We will not need to ask because He knows we are thankful in every situation. He will simply begin to make every provision in a timely manner. God is happy when we praise, worship, honor, and glorify Him. We are simply telling Him that there is nothing He cannot do.

After we have done all of the above, then we can channel our petition to God in faith believing that He is a prayer answering God. Nothing is new under the sun. Every problem we face today was once somebody else's problem in the Bible. That is to say that some individual who lived before us suffered that same affliction and the Bible provides us the solution to the affliction. As we read and meditate on the Word of God, we get inspiration as to how to stand upon the Word of God and pray according to our circumstances.

The Bible says that God has lifted His word above His own name. This means that if we pray according to His word, we should expect answers to our prayers. When we go through family challenges, we should search for a word in the Bible that speaks to our situation and stand upon it and pray, and God, who has lifted His word above His own name, will honor His word.

Each time we profess God and follow Him, our thought patterns should be renewed as stated in the book of Romans. Our thinking should divert from that of the people of the world who believe in nothing but their strength, intelligence, money, and power.

The devil wants the people of God to think and act like the people of the world rather than being deeply rooted in the Word of God and making positive confessions based on what the word of God says. The enemy will influence us through the voices we listen to, be they music lyrics, or some Christian friends who still speak the language of the world, but we should rather speak and act as commanded in

Romans 12:2 (KJV):

"And be not conformed to this world: but be ye transformed by the renewing of your mind, that ye may prove what is that good, and acceptable, and perfect, will of God."

Moreover, in Philippians 4:8(KJV) the word of God encourages us thus:

"Finally, brethren, whatsoever things are true, whatsoever things are honest, whatsoever things are just, whatsoever things are pure, whatsoever things are lovely, whatsoever things are of good report; if there be any virtue, and if there be any praise, think on these things."

The Power of Faith

God is a spirit, and He made us in His image, meaning that we have spirits, and therefore, we can connect with Him through our spirit. Faith is the vehicle that will take us on this journey. God promised He will never leave us nor forsake us, so no matter how deep the ditch in which we find ourselves, He will surely bring us out. I thank God every day when I wake up because I know my life is in His hands, and no terrifying situation makes me tremble. I call on the name of Jesus, and the solution will surely come.

CHAPTER SEVEN

The Growth of Our Faith

After examining and analyzing the importance of faith in our lives as Christians, it goes without saying that the greatest gift we need to pray for is the gift of faith. When we pray, we should believe that our prayer has already been answered. Prayer is conversing with God, therefore, it takes faith to pray to a God that you do not see and have never seen. The foundation of our faith is love. The Bible says:

"For God so loved the world, that he gave his only begotten Son, that whosoever believeth in him should not perish, but have everlasting life." John 3:16(KJV)

If children of the world can trust that their parents will provide for them because they love them, in like manner Christians should trust God who is the Creator and is better than earthly parents in every aspect. We ought to believe in the work of creation. We are not here on earth because of our physical parents. God ordained that we should be created before bringing our parents to each other.

The Power of Faith

"Before I formed thee in the belly I knew thee; and before thou camest forth out of the womb I sanctified thee, and I ordained thee a prophet unto the nations". Jeremiah 1:5(KJV)

The only way to make the burdens we bear lighter is to call upon God because that is the way He meant for things to be. He made us out of love and has good plans for us, but in order that these plans should be accomplished, we must recognize His existence and acknowledge the fact that our intelligence and personal talents by themselves cannot provide us good success and a fulfilled life.

God has to be in it for our success and joy to be complete. God created us to communicate with Him, to praise and worship Him so that He can in turn bless and protect us. This is impossible if we don't have faith in God. He loves us so much that He gave each one of us a certain measure of faith which we are expected to nourish through the Word of God. Although the devil messed with the original plan of God for our lives in the Garden of Eden, by causing Adam and Eve to fall into sin, God quickly redeemed us from total condemnation by sending us His son Jesus to pay the price and reconcile us to Him. This is why we should continue to magnify His name even in the midst of our difficulties because His mercy is unfathomable, and His love knows no end.

It is His wish for all His children to be set free from every bondage in which we find ourselves. He wants every lost sheep to be brought back into the fold. His greatest wish is to see the very last sinner repent before His return.

"Likewise, I say unto you, there is joy in the presence of the angels of God over one sinner that repenteth." Luke 15:10 (KJV)

"Therefore say unto the house of Israel, Thus saith the Lord God; Repent, and turn yourselves from your idols; and turn away your faces from all your abomination" Ezekiel 14:6(KJV)

God addresses the people of Israel in this manner not only because He is a jealous God but also because He is the only one who can do with our lives as He pleases. He gave us life, and He can take it anytime, anywhere, and anyhow. Today, this same message goes to you and I, who were born into the kingdom of God through His son's death on the cross. We should be mindful of turning our spouses, our wealth, our jobs, our children, and our career positions into idols that take the place of God in our lives. These persons and things are good and make our lives easier, more comfortable, and more interesting here on earth, but God ought to occupy the first place in the life of every Christian. This can only be achieved when we communicate with our Heavenly Father continuously through His word to increase our faith.

"So then faith cometh by hearing, and hearing by the word of God." Romans 10:17(KJV):

As we spend time in the word of God we should equally covert the Holy Spirit to help us reach that level of spiritually where we truly put God first in all areas of our lives. We can't do it by our power or might. God is restating His faithfulness and His love for us:

"That the house of Israel may go no more astray from me, neither be polluted any more with all their transgressions; but that they may be my people, and I may be their God, saith the Lord God." Ezekiel 6:11(KJV)

We cannot live our lives worshipping idols and expect God to intervene in our circumstances when we find our backs against the wall. Although grace abounds where sin prevails, God is a holy God, and therefore, He does not like sin. God wants our full attention so that when the counsel of the wicked gathers against us, He can sit in heaven and look at them and laugh. He can do to us like He did for Job. - No matter the affliction we go through, we can neither give the glory that belongs to Him to idols nor to man. We must be fully committed, trust God with everything we have, and this will attract His attention on us and His wrath upon our enemies: As we do this, then in the day of trouble, God can say to us like he said to King Jehoshaphat:

"And he said, Hearken ye, all Judah, and ye inhabitants of Jerusalem, and thou king Jehoshaphat, Thus saith the Lord unto you, Be not afraid nor dismayed by reason of this great multitude; for the battle is not yours, but God>s." 2 Chronicles 20:15(KJV)

When God gave this prophesy to King Jehoshaphat, it came to pass because of the covenant of faith the king had with Him. God is no respecter of persons. What He does for one, He is able to do for all. The requirement is for us to grow our faith to the level where we know beyond all reasonable doubt that God can never fail us as long as we continue to walk according to His statutes.

The God that we serve is a talking God. He speaks to His people all the time. The most common way through which He speaks to us is through His word, but he also speaks to us through other people even those we sometimes tend to despise or undermine. Every child of God must develop high sensitivity in the spirit. Our minds are too small to imagine how, when, and where God can decide to give us a mind blowing experience. The best way is to stay tuned to Him, sharpen our spiritual antennae, and become highly sensitive in the spirit.

Our faith is the master key that will open every door that God has planted on the road to our destiny. It is our faith that will turn God's promises to reality.

The Bible is very rich and loaded with words to encourage us and build our faith. In reality, it is easy to say with our mouths that we trust God, but when we go through a series of afflictions that do not seem to end, our faith is shaken to the point where we begin to ask questions and even doubt the very existence of God.

Each time we find ourselves in such overwhelming circumstances, we need to rise up with great determination to pray and spend more time in the Word of God in order to hear His voice. Are you going through a stormy situation in your life at this moment? God will hold your hand and give you direction. Listen to what God is saying in Deuteronomy 31:6(KJV)

"Be strong and of a good courage, fear not, nor be afraid of them: for the Lord thy God, he it is that doth go with thee; he will not fail thee, nor forsake thee."

The Power of Faith

These words which He spoke to Joshua in the Old Testament are the same words that He is speaking to you and me today. We are the Joshua generation of our time. We war against personal and societal challenges every day, and in order to remain focused, strong ,and peaceful we ought to meditate on the instructions God gave us in Joshua 1:6-9 (KJV)

"Be strong and of a good courage: for unto this people shalt thou divide for an inheritance the land, which I sware unto their fathers to give them.7 Only be thou strong and very courageous, that thou mayest observe to do according to all the law, which Moses my servant commanded thee: turn not from it to the right hand or to the left, that thou mayest prosper withersoever thou goest.

⁸This book of the law shall not depart out of thy mouth; but thou shalt meditate therein day and night, that thou mayest observe to do according to all that is written therein: for then thou shalt make thy way prosperous, and then thou shalt have good success.

⁹Have not I commanded thee? Be strong and of a good courage; be not afraid, neither be thou dismayed: for the Lord thy God is with thee whithersoever thou goest."

We notice many words repeating themselves in this passage. God is emphasizing the fact that no one can challenge or question His authority and His dominion. When He tells you to move, you should be confident and have no fear because He is more than able to defend you in your time of calamity.

When you go make sure God is ahead of you, never after you. God's words will break every yoke, destroy every demon, renew our strength, and encourage us.

Who is the strong man or strong woman in your family, at your job, in your finances, or in your health that has drawn a line that you cannot cross to the next level? Is the enemy using your loved ones to torment your life and cause you to despair? Have you exhausted your energy and resources to the point of giving up? Do you feel like the whole world is against you? Is your mean supervisor refusing to promote you in spite of your hard work and qualification because he/she is clinging unto their favorites who are buying their promotions with sweet talk? Your God is bigger than all those battles you are facing.

"Ye shall not need to fight in this battle: set yourselves, stand ye still, and see the salvation of the Lord with you, O Judah and Jerusalem: fear not, nor be dismayed; tomorrow go out against them: for the Lord will be with you." 2 Chronicles 20:17(KJV)

David was a man after Gods heart because he had tasted of God's love goodness, and faithfulness. So he knew how to run to God and cry out to Him any time he faced challenges. He also knew how to go on his knees and repent genuinely when he had wronged God because he had no other God. David's faith was the currency he used to purchase the grace of God he needed to win every battle and overcome every obstacle.

"You are my hiding place from every storm of life; You even keep me from getting into trouble! You surround me with songs of victory. I will instruct you (says the Lord) and guide you along the best pathway for your life; I will advise you and watch your progress. Don't be like a senseless horse or mule that has to have a bit in its mouth to keep it in line!" Psalms 32:7-9: (KJV)

Many Christians go through a period of discouragement. They have prayed, fasted, given towards the work of God, to the poor and the needy, and are trying to live righteous lives. Yet, the answers they are expecting from God are not coming. At this time, they look around and see people who do not know or profess God living what they think are happy and successful lives. These unbelievers may have money, drive expensive cars, or live in mansions, but they may not have the peace and good health they need to make their joy complete. We should learn not to look at others as better or more blessed than we are, because that can make us discouraged to the point where we begin to question God. God never forgets His people. He is looking at your heart and working things out for your good.

"Rest in the Lord, and wait patiently for him: fret not thyself because of him who prospereth in his way, because of the man who bringeth wicked devices to pass." Psalms 37:7 (KJV).

"I waited patiently for the Lord; and he inclined unto me, and heard my cry. 2 He brought me up also out of an horrible pit, out of the miry clay, and set my feet upon a rock, and established my goings.3 And he hath put a new song in my mouth, even praise unto our God: many shall see it, and fear, and shall trust in the Lord". Psalm 40:1-3(KJV)

It is easy to praise and worship God when everything is going well in our lives. In the days of trials, temptations, pain, desperation, disappointments, uncertainties, anxieties, afflictions, and hardship we fall back and ask questions. There will always be difficult times in the life of every one of us. We may never really be able to say where the problem is coming from or why it is coming, but the one thing we should continue to confess is that it will go away. God is always watching over us and has promised never to leave us nor abandon us. He always shows up at the right time.

We all can agree that it is truly difficult to praise God when you don't have a roof over your head, or when you are hungry but can neither afford a meal for yourself nor for your family. Look at what the Apostle Paul wrote here:

"Not that I speak in respect of want: for I have learned, in whatsoever state I am, therewith to be content.

[12]I know both how to be abased, and I know how to abound: everywhere and in all things I am instructed both to be full and to be hungry, both to abound and to suffer need.

[13]I can do all things through Christ which strengtheneth me." Philippians 4:11-13(KJV)

Maybe you or someone in your family just got a bad medical report from the doctor. I wouldd like to reiterate that God is The Ancient of Days. He was in existence before the beginning. He alone is constant in an ever changing world. He is the ALPHA and the OMEGA. In times of sickness, let's go back to His word and make reference to the instances where Jesus healed the sick. It is important here to highlight the fact that those who got their healing were those that believed and had faith that God was able to heal them. The woman with the issue of blood kept pressing through the crowd. Why would she do that if she wasn't sure of the end result? Our faith will grant us entry into every door we need to enter as we journey with God. We are not undermining the importance of western medicine.

We acknowledge the fact that God inspires pharmacists and medical doctors to invent medications and methods to treat certain diseases. If God decides not to do an instant miracle for us, He will still be able to guide us to the right doctor and give that doctor the inspiration to give us the correct diagnosis and treatment. In order for this to happen, we need to have a relationship with God, be prayerful, and have faith in God.

"20 And, behold, a woman, which was diseased with an issue of blood twelve years, came behind him, and touched the hem of his garment:

[21]For she said within herself, If I may but touch his garment, I shall be whole.

[22]But Jesus turned him about, and when he saw her, he said, Daughter, be of good comfort; thy faith hath made thee whole. And the woman was made whole from that hour."(Matt9:20-22KJV)

The opposing crowd we face today in our own lives is not a human crowd but the spirit of doubt. We have to push and force the spirit of doubt out in order to find ourselves in the presence of God like the woman with the issue of blood.

In the presence of God, every problem will bow. Every evil spirit will flee.

When we read the story of David and Goliath in the book of 1 Samuel 17, we see that the Philistines gathered their armies together at Sokoh in Judah to fight against the children of Israel. Goliath was massive and over nine feet tall. Goliath was dressed in a bronze armor from head to toe with all kinds of arms ready to destroy anyone that would dare to challenge him.

The Israelites were scared by his size and his armor. For several days, Goliath continued to terrorize the Israelites until one morning when David was around to give food to three of his older brothers. David noticed the terror Goliath was causing the people of Israel. Even King Saul was greatly troubled by this situation. When David saw Goliath come out to defy Israel again, he had this to say:

"And David spake to the men that stood by him, saying, What shall be done to the man that killeth this Philistine, and taketh away the reproach from Israel? for who is this uncircumcised Philistine, that he should defy the armies of the living God?"(1 Samuel 17:26 KJV).

David informed King Saul that he was going to fight Goliath, but the king was scared because David was smaller and had no armor. When David insisted, the king gave him his coat of armor and bronze helmet for his head, but it was too big. However, David decided to go against the Philistine.

"David said moreover, The Lord that delivered me out of the paw of the lion, and out of the paw of the bear, he will deliver me out of the hand of this Philistine. And Saul said unto David, Go, and the Lord be with thee.(1 Samuel 17:37 KJV)"

David knew that he had no armor and that Goliath was bigger, taller, and was backed by a very strong army but this did not shaken him. He knew the God he was serving. His God was bigger than Goliath, and the hosts of angels standing with the children of Israel were more than the army of the Philistines. Every time children of God are in battle ,they are accompanied by a host of angels. We need to see these angels with our spiritual eyes all the time and expect victory. This is how we work our faith and chase the enemy out of our territory. God does not give us what we do not see with our spiritual eyes.

"Then said David to the Philistine, Thou comest to me with a sword, and with a spear, and with a shield: but I come to thee in the name of the Lord of hosts, the God of the armies of Israel, whom thou hast defied.

This day will the Lord deliver thee into mine hand; and I will smite thee, and take thine head from thee; and I will give the carcases of the host of the Philistines this day unto the fowls of the air, and to the wild beasts of the earth; that all the earth may know that there is a God in Israel. And all this assembly shall know that the Lord saveth not with sword and spear: for the battle is the Lord's, and he will give you into our hands. 1 Samuel 17:45-47(KJV).

David was the youngest of the sons of Jesse and spent his time tending the sheep in the wilderness. On many occasions God saved him from destruction from the mouths of lions and bears. This grew his faith and made him to trust God fully.

"And David put his hand in his bag, and took thence a stone, and slang it, and smote the Philistine in his forehead, that the stone sunk into his forehead; and he fell upon his face to the earth. So David prevailed over the Philistine with a sling and with a stone, and smote the Philistine, and slew him; but there was no sword in the hand of David."(1 Samuel 17:48-50KJV)

The story of the victory of David over Goliath is a clear indication that when we replace fear with faith we can cause God to manifest His power and glory through us. God has called many of us to be like David in our families, our communities, and our nations. Until we banish fear, strengthen our faith, take up our stones and slings, and get on the offensive, the enemy will continue to feast on our blessings. This is the only means by which we will accomplish the mission that has been assigned to us. We should stop relying on our physical weapons, knowing that our battles are spiritual and that we are not wrestling against flesh and blood but against principalities and powers.

Many of the Philistines in the camp of Goliath and even some Israelites who were listening to David would have been wondering if he was in his right mind. Others would have been laughing out loud. It is the same today when we proclaim our faith or make some declarations by faith. Some of the people around us who do not believe in the omnipotence of God may make a mockery of us; others will label us as frustrated and disappointed fanatics. Never let these voices dampen your faith. Stay focused on God, and He will come through for you.

He will defend His name and His grace shall be made manifest in your situation at the appointed time. Never let any Goliath slaying opportunity pass you by. Have your stones ever ready, stones that are heavily coated with faith, and like David, go against them in the name of your God.

Faith grows best under attack. When we pray for God to take away our problems, we are indirectly saying that we don't want to grow spiritually because even those failures can contribute to our spiritual growth. The story of Daniel, Shadrach, Meshach, and Abednego is another outstanding example of faith in display. The thing I find very impressive about this story in the book of Daniel is their unity and determination. They found themselves in captivity under King Nebuchadnezzar and received all kinds of threats, but not once did they deviate from their faith and their trust in the power of their God. They worked as a team. If each of them had decided to respond or react in their own way, the enemy could have prevailed over them.

I would, at this point, like to emphasize the importance of unity in group prayers in our families, our churches, and other organizations. The devil is very cunning and he knows that God has stated that where two or three are gathered in His name He is in their midst.

Every time there is a gathering of the children of God he will always find a way to intrude. Sometimes he can use some of the members of the group to accomplish his wicked plans. It is, therefore, of the utmost importance to pray for the spirit of oneness each time we gather as a group. God does not like discord, so it is difficult for the Holy Spirit to flow where division thrives.

"But Daniel purposed in his heart that he would not defile himself with the portion of the king's meat, nor with the wine which he drank: therefore he requested of the prince of the eunuchs that he might not defile himself." Daniel 1:8 (KJV)

When Daniel decided that he was not eating the meat from King Nebuchadnezzar, the other three followed suit. God showed up in their situation because they worked in one spirit. Daniel was aware of what was at stake if he defiled himself with the king's meat. He knew he was serving the King of Kings and did not want to compromise his relationship with the great "I AM".

Furthermore, he believed God was able to grant him every request. King Nebuchadnezzar was about to destroy all the seers including Daniel, Shadrach, Meshach, and Abednego because they could not give him an interpretation for his dream. What did Daniel do?

He asked for time to seek the face of God because he knew He was the King in heaven, the one who reveals secret things. After Daniel prayed, God gave him the interpretation of the king's dream. This is how they found favor with the King.

"[16]Then Daniel went in, and desired of the king that he would give him time, and that he would shew the king the interpretation.

The Power of Faith

¹⁷Then Daniel went to his house, and made the thing known to Hananiah, Mishael, and Azariah, his companions:

¹⁸That they would desire mercies of the God of heaven concerning this secret; that Daniel and his fellows should not perish with the rest of the wise men of Babylon.

¹⁹Then was the secret revealed unto Daniel in a night vision. Then Daniel blessed the God of heaven.

²⁰Daniel answered and said, Blessed be the name of God for ever and ever: for wisdom and might are his:

²¹And he changeth the times and the seasons: he removeth kings, and setteth up kings: he giveth wisdom unto the wise, and knowledge to them that know understanding:

²²He revealeth the deep and secret things: he knoweth what is in the darkness, and the light dwelleth with him.

²³I thank thee, and praise thee, O thou God of my fathers, who hast given me wisdom and might, and hast made known unto me now what we desired of thee: for thou hast now made known unto us the king's matter." Daniel 2:16-22(KJV)

Daniel is showing us how people of faith ought to seek solutions to their problems. They should go into their prayer closets, place the request on the altar of God, and have a conversation with Him. Daniel did not call some friend to complain, he did not ask someone to pray so that they should be set free. He went directly to God first, because he had a relationship with Him, and because he had confidence in his God. It is important for us to have a relationship with

God. He is pleased with us when we call upon Him always just to tell Him how great He is. This prepares the ground for us so that in time of trouble when we call, He intervenes and does what every father does to defend his children. When we are wholeheartedly connected to Him and give Him complete responsibility and authority over our lives, we can rest assured that He will always show up to rescue us.

"⁵Trust in the Lord with all thine heart; and lean not unto thine own understanding.6 In all thy ways acknowledge him, and he shall direct thy paths." Proverbs 3:5-6 (KJV)

"Consider it pure joy, my brothers and sisters, whenever you face trials of many kinds, 3 because you know that the testing of your faith produces perseverance. 4 Let perseverance finish its work so that you may be mature and complete, not lacking anything." James 1:2-4 (KJV)

It is true that God sent Jesus to set us free, but He sometimes allows us to go through challenges, either to bring us closer to Him or so that we can better appreciate His greatness and his mighty hand when He shows up powerfully in our circumstances.

On many occasions in the Bible, God warns us about fear. He repeatedly told Joshua," Fear not" as he led the children of Israel after Moses died. Fear is the killer of faith. It is a natural reaction to unforeseen, unexpected, and unpleasant circumstances, but we should quickly speak words of faith and encouragement to such situations. There is power in our tongues, and we should learn to exercise this authority in times of difficulty. The Bible says we shall declare a thing and it shall come to pass. If we declare a good thing, it comes to pass. Similarly, if we declare a negative thing it shall come to pass. As Christians, we should renew our minds every day and speak positive words in every situation concerning our lives, our children, family members, friends, and everyone around us.

"Cast not away therefore your confidence, which hath great recompence of reward.

For ye have need of patience, that, after ye have done the will of God, ye might receive the promise.

For yet a little while, and he that shall come will come, and will not tarry.

Now the just shall live by faith: but if any man draws back, my soul shall have no pleasure in him." Hebrews 10:35-38 (KJV)

In this passage, our Heavenly Father is warning some of us who are impatient to be careful, that having done the will of God we may lose the reward that awaits us because of our impatience. Our confidence in God is what will be rewarded both while we are here on Earth and in Heaven.

God has endowed us all with gifts of the Spirit but it is the fruits of the Spirit which will sustain these gifts. These gifts will help us to flourish and remain strong in the fight against the enemy who is always trying to pull us back. When we display our gift publicly in order to prove a point we risk grieving the Holy Spirit. If there is an imbalance and immaturity in the practice of spiritual gifts we could be making a mockery of the Spirit of God. If we value the gifts of the spirit more than the fruit of the spirit we can become abusive in the operation of our spiritual gifts.

Galatians 5:22 (KJV) tells us what these fruits are:

"^{22}But the fruit of the Spirit is love, joy, peace, longsuffering, gentleness, goodness, faith,

^{23}Meekness, temperance: against such there is no law."

Love is the first of them because where there is love the rest of the fruits will clearly manifest with little or no effort. When we begin to operate in these gifts, and portray the fruits in our daily lives, the enemy can no longer manipulate us because our maturity in the Spirit puts God in total control over our lives. In other words, we come to the end of self and just give over the whole work of making us what we ought to be to the indwelling Holy Spirit. Then, and only then, holy graces of character are His fruit. This balance and spiritual maturity is acquired by faith and also as we spend time in the word of God and in His presence. We must daily seek His face and love Him by spreading His love to all those around us.

An important reminder here is for Christians to stop counting the number of years during which they have been baptized or born again and start looking at how the fruits of the Spirit are mirrored in their daily interaction with other human beings both in the world and in the church. This is an important yardstick for measuring one who has walked meticulously with God.

Chapter Eight

Faith, Fear, and Discouragement.

Finally, as children of God, we need to pray against the spirit of fear every day. This spirit of fear may not come from within us, especially when we are already deeply rooted in the Word of God. As cunning as the enemy is, he can decide to use anyone around us, be they our parents, our siblings, our spouses, our children, our colleagues, our neighbors, and clients. We have to know the people we surround ourselves with and pray for the spirit of discernment to be able to distinguish the voice of God from that of the enemy. God's voice will never frighten us and will never take away our peace. Besides, God assures us that He has not given us a spirit of fear.

"For God hath not given us the spirit of fear; but of power, and of love, and of a sound mind." 2 Timothy 1:7(KJV)

He is the God of mercy and compassion, and no matter how much we have annoyed Him, His arms are always open to receive a repentant sinner. We should never think we are too sinful to go to God. All we need is to be truly repentant.

"18 There is no fear in love; but perfect love casteth out fear: because fear hath torment. He that feareth is not made perfect in love." 1 John 4:18 (KJV)

When we read the story of Job we see an account of a righteous man, who was upright and God- fearing. God gave Satan the permission to torment Job but warned him not to touch his soul. These tribulations started when Job was afflicted with boils all over his body. He was in terrible pain, but instead of consoling and comforting Job, his own wife uttered words of discouragement. She had forgotten of all the blessings from God.

"Then said his wife unto him, Dost thou still retain thine integrity? curse God, and die.

10 But he said unto her, Thou speakest as one of the foolish women speaketh. What? shall we receive good at the hand of God, and shall we not receive evil? In all this did not Job sin with his lips." Job 2:9-10(KJV)

We should always guard against what people around us say when it comes to our relationship with God. Job suffered material and human losses, and although he cried and spent sleepless nights, he never forgot to give God the highest place.

He was convinced that no one else could do for him what God had done and was still able to do.

"For the arrows of the Almighty are within me, the poison whereof drinketh up my spirit: the terrors of God do set themselves in array against me. " Job 6:4(KJV)

In the rest of this chapter, and chapter seven, he laments in desperation as he was overwhelmed by his troubles. While he was going through these tribulations, his own friends who should have encouraged him, were increasing his pain by telling him that it was he sin that made God decide to punish him.

"Then answered Bildad the Shuhite, and said,

² How long wilt thou speak these things? and how long shall the words of thy mouth be like a strong wind?

³ Doth God pervert judgment? or doth the Almighty pervert justice?

⁴ If thy children have sinned against him, and he have cast them away for their transgression;

⁵ If thou wouldest seek unto God betimes, and make thy supplication to the Almighty;

⁶ If thou wert pure and upright; surely now he would awake for thee, and make the habitation of thy righteousness prosperous." Job 8:1-6(KJV)

These are the voices of discouragement we are talking about. Job's wife and friends stood up against his faith. If he had listened to them, he would never have been restored.

Even in the church today, some brethren not only refuse to empathize with you when you go through challenges, but they say negative things about you and conclude that it is your sin that is causing you suffering and pain.

Sometimes God just wants to chastise His children out of love, and it is not the place of any human being to draw any conclusions about our case.

We should be like Job who said, even after God tarried in taking away his pain that, he was still going to exalt His name and continue to trust Him. The only way to achieve this is to shut our ears to these voices of obstruction and cry out for mercy and grace to respond only to the voice of God alone.

Ungratefulness can obstruct our blessings. Each time we go before God, we ought to go with a spirit of thanksgiving. In ordinary life, we are happy when someone says "thank you" for a service rendered or when we give them a gift. These are the people who are likely to attract our attention subsequently. The same goes for our beloved Master and Lord Jesus. In the passage that follows, in Luke 17, faith was at work again here as we hear Jesus tell the lepers that their faith has healed them of leprosy.

However, it is worth noting that the one leper who exhibited both great faith and appreciation is the one that received the most from Jesus. The other nine had faith and were healed of leprosy, but because they were not thankful, because they never went back to Jesus to show appreciation, they were never made completely whole.

"[12]And as he entered into a certain village, there met him ten men that were lepers, which stood afar off:

[13]And they lifted up their voices, and said, Jesus, Master, have mercy on us.

¹⁴And when he saw them, he said unto them, Go shew yourselves unto the priests. And it came to pass, that, as they went, they were cleansed.

¹⁵And one of them, when he saw that he was healed, turned back, and with a loud voice glorified God,

¹⁶And fell down on his face at his feet, giving him thanks: and he was a Samaritan.

¹⁷And Jesus answering said, Were there not ten cleansed? but where are the nine?

¹⁸There are not found that returned to give glory to God, save this stranger.

¹⁹And he said unto him, Arise, go thy way: thy faith hath made thee whole." Luke 17:12-19 (KJV)

The lesson we learn here is that Jesus is more interested in people who show a thankful attitude towards Him especially when they receive a miracle. We also learn that we should never let any negative force stand against our faith. Our faith must help us to overcome all other forces that tend to interfere when our faith is in motion.

Some of these negative forces speak against our giving to God. Why should we give to God? As earlier indicated, God is a giver because He gave us the most precious gift: His only son.

We can't call Him Father and refuse to give. Every child has inherited traits from the parents. We should learn to give back to God, and our brethren, to qualify to be called children of God. Again we should give as a sign of humility to acknowledge He is the owner of everything here on Earth. Thirdly we should give as a sign of appreciation to our Father to tell Him that all we have has been given to us by God.

Then we are standing upon the Word that says that when we give it shall be given back to us. One of the ways to touch God's heart is by giving, especially towards the propagation of the Gospel, and to the needy.

We should never allow ourselves to be derailed by the voices that discourage us from giving. Nobody has ever carried their wealth with them to their graves. It makes no sense to have huge sums of money and see people go hungry around you. God always blesses us so that we should be a blessing to those who are less privileged. Children of God should note that giving warms the heart of God.

As children of God, we don't want to miss out on any blessings. Every time God is moving, we want to be in the spirit so that He will not pass us by. The first step towards achieving this goal is to establish a viable relationship with Master Jesus. This relationship must be grounded on, sustained, and galvanized by a deeply rooted and unshakable faith.

"But the scripture hath concluded all under sin that, the promise by faith of Jesus Christ might be given to them that believe." Galatians 3:22(KJV)

This scripture is telling us that everything we receive from God is based on our faith, so brethren, as we move forward, we must take this seriously and watch over our faith keenly because when the enemy attacks and weakens our faith, we can't communicate or receive from God. This is the time we may fall back and begin to question God. Let's pray for God's grace to help us never to fall in this trap.

It is my fervent prayer that everyone who reads this book shall establish a relationship, deeply rooted in faith in God. This relationship should be nourished, and galvanized with prayers, and meditation on the Word of God, so that you can be mightily blessed in the mighty name of Jesus!

Prayers of Faith

- Lord Jesus, I come before you today like a repentant sinner, to ask you to forgive me all my sins. I accept you as my personal Lord and Savior, and I invite you to come and dwell in my heart today and always. In the mighty name of Jesus Amen!

- My Father, my God, you conquer the darkness of ignorance by the light of your Word. Strengthen within our hearts the faith you have given us; let not temptation ever quench the fire that your love has kindled within us. By faith we have trusted in you. Grant that as we daily seek your face, the yokes in our lives will be broken, the evil arrows fired into our lives shall be fired back to their senders, every closed door of opportunity shall be opened and every evil word spoken by the enemy over our lives shall be reversed in the mighty name of Jesus. Amen!

- Mighty and Everlasting Father, we thank you for loving us unconditionally. We are grateful because we can come boldly to the mercy seat because of your faithfulness. We love you because you first loved us and demonstrated your love by sending your only son to die a shameful death in order to reconcile us to you. Father, grant us the grace to love you in return by loving your word which you have lifted above your own name. Grant us the grace to study your word and learn to stand upon it in times of tribulations, afflictions, and temptations. As overcomers, may you sustain us and help us stay in every fight till the final round to appropriate the victory Jesus purchased for us on the cross. Amen!

ABOUT THE AUTHOR

Mrs. Emmerentia Nupa Asafor was born in the village of Akum, in the North West Region of Cameroon. Emmerentia's " The Power of Faith" is about her more than 15 years of personal experience in an intimate relationship with God. She is greatly in love with God, and enjoys sharing her faith experiences with everyone she comes in contact with. She is an Ambassador for Christ, and a powerful prayer warrior, who believes strongly in the miracle power of God, through prayers. She now worships in the powerful, and dynamic, DUNAMIS WORSHIP CHAPEL INTERNATIONAL, in Maryland, USA, under the leadership of Prophet Pascal Kamgang.

Emmerentia's greatest desire is for you to experience the same powerful love experience she has with God as you read this book. She is currently a school teacher in Maya Angelou, French Immersion, Middle Scholl, in PG County MD.

Among her academic achievements are:

DFLE, from CLA, Besancon, France; MA Bilingual Education, Yaounde; MA English Language, Yaounde; and DEA , English Language Studies, University of Yaounde.

With over 25 years of teaching experience, 13 of them have been in the US, where she holds multiple teaching certifications, and became an accomplished teacher of French in the US when she obtained the National Board Certification in the State of Maryland in 2013.

She likes working with children, and enjoys helping build their future as she watches their lives transform one day at a time.

Notes

The Power of Faith

Notes

Emmerentia Nupa Asafor

Notes

Made in the USA
San Bernardino, CA
05 February 2018